A
COLLECTION OF POEMS

ADA OSAJI

ISBN: 979-8-688-47530-2

ACKNOWLEDGMENTS

To God be all the glory.

Authors and poets alike, may seem simple, but require lots of support and love. Ada's Collection of Poems would not have been possible without these lovely people.

Grandma Victoria, the poet. She wrote many poems over the years, but didn't save them in a collection. When she realized I loved writing, she told me to keep them in all file, write the date and to make a note to remind myself of my source of inspiration.

Kimberly - My dear cousin, whose poetry inspired two poems of my own.

Sara - A constant inspiration, best pal and friend. We bounced poetry ideas off each other in fifth grade. Most of my poems were written about school and life. Sara helped me find topics and even encouraged me to write.

Ms. Greer and Mr. Hallet, my two wonderful 5th grade teachers - these teachers first introduced me to the world of writing poetry, breaking down the concepts, and helping me with my poems. These teachers deserve all the credit they can get.

Thank you to Mr. Back, my sixth grade English, Language Arts teacher, who encouraged me to keep on writing and to share my writing with others.

Natalie Wambui - A girl my age published her own book of poems. I saw her speaking to a large audience about her books. "No need to wait for some time in the future," my mother said.

Ms. Pam - My nanny (and adopted grandma) who helped me with homework and even read some of my upcoming books.

My parents, without whom this book would not have been possible.

Love always, my friends and family.

AUTHOR'S NOTE

Dear readers,

I was six years old when I memorized The Schoolroom Clock by Mother Goose for a first grade poetry competition in Peoria, Illinois. I did so well representing my class and got a blue ribbon. All the parents and teachers gathered in the school gym for the final presentation.

My name was picked from a hat. I stood in front of the microphone before the audience, wondering what I was supposed to do. I leaned over and asked the lady standing next to me what she wanted me to do. She told me that I should say my speech. I thanked her, and said it as best I could to the large audience. Lots of people came to acknowledge me afterwards. My school principal congratulated me. I didn't know he knew my name! He said, I did a great job. It was awesome and so inspiring. I have competed in all the ACSI (Association of Christian Schools) Speech Meet competitions up to the fourth grade when it was discontinued. I wrote these poems during my fifth and sixth grade years.

Thank you to all the teachers, students and parents who work hard to create these moments that inspire a little girl to love poetry and even try to write.

The Schoolroom Clock By Mother Goose
(My First Grade Speech)

There's a neat little clock,
in the schoolroom it stands,
and it points to the time,
with its two little hands.
And may we, like the clock keep a face clean and bright,
with hands ever ready,
i to do what is right.

CONTENTS

The Continent Where You Are 1

A Good Morrow 2

Busy, Busy Bee 3

Inspiration 4

In Grandma's House 6

Predators and Prey 8

What A Bore 10

Beyblades 12

If Comfort Mattered More Than Happiness 15

Call of the Wild 17

Bullying 20

Forever Friends 23

Imagination 25

THE CONTINENT WHERE YOU ARE

If every continent could get along,

Give a hug,

Share a song

They would give up fights,

Turn around,

Do what's right

If only they knew what to say

Something nice,

In the right way

Just let the world see,

We're the same As can be,

If someone could smile as bright as a star,

It would lighten up

The continent where you are.

A Good Morrow

When all the humans are gone,
Though they won't be for long.
The teacups bounce out
With vigorous prancing
and joyous shouts
Out of the drawer
Onto the floor
Trying not to crack,
Jumping off the rack.
They throw some raisins in the air
And eat pieces off a big green pear.
Click!
Click!
Click!
The humans are back!
Back to the drawer, Back to the rack! Though parting gives
them sorrow,
They still wish each other,
A good morrow.

BUSY, BUSY BEE

How fast,
how slow,
How high,
and low.
Oh, where did he go?
Busy bee
bumps right into me!
How big was he?
I didn't see!
Busy bee
Oh, but why me? Couldn't he fly To Hawaii?
Busy bee
Round and round he chases me, Then finally crashes into a tree
Yes, I'm free,
he lost me!
What a busy bee!

INSPIRATION

It dawns on you,
Like a cloud
ready to burst, To pour it's rain,
To quench your thirst
To spread it's love
to everyone,
Different and alike.
To find your purpose,
To do what's right
Oh, inspiration,
you are too beautiful
for anyone to see
So keen and clear,
like an eagle's eye,
So flawless
you just know.
You don't ever wonder why
You can't hear it,
Or see it,
But you know its there,

It's in your heart,

It's everywhere

Oh, inspiration,

Like a light in the darkness A flower ready to bloom,

A cheetah ready to zoom, To catch its prey

To feed it's cubs

Until they grow strong,

And know right from wrong Oh, inspiration!

Where are you, they say? Well inspiration is right here, On this very page.

In Grandma's House

In Grandma's House,
every pot and pan is filled with delicious food.
It makes me have a happy face, and lightens up my mood.
Every plate and every platter
Is cleaned with water, and splatter

In Grandma's house,
She is a teacher.
She helps with schoolwork too!
In grandma's house,
We read a poem or fable.
We always read,
on the couch or table.
We all know Grandma rules!

In Grandma's house,
there is much much more,
That she has set for you in store.
You cannot leave my Grandma's House Without a gift or
present,

Not like a fancy picture

or coffee mug,

Her favorite is a hug.

I wrote this poem for my Grandmother's 80th birthday and family reunion, in Nigeria. I didn't get to say it for her at the big event party, but it was published in the program for the event.

PREDATORS AND PREY

Running here
Running there
almost running,
everywhere.
Under bushes,
slinking in shadows,
in the darkness,
as dark as sparrows.
Glistening black fur,
a growl,
not even as close as a purr.
A silent moment,
then a chase to the end.
For getting food you cannot spend.
Animals have to learn how to stick together.
For they will be protected,
for now, but not forever.
It's always a battle,
a challenge you see,
to find food,

as easy as he.
If you were an animal,
what would you try?
Would you stick together,
as close as a pride?
A predator is much harder to be.
Without them,
where would be,
the little cubs at the zoo you see?

WHAT A BORE

What a bore!
Every time.
Makes me snore.
Reading time
Waiting more.
Time to rhyme.

Math is the worst.
People actually sleep.
Makes me want to burst.
But you have to do it without a peep.

At last the bell rings
and then you feel your heart lift
You want to rise up and sing.
The class runs out very swift.
To the next class you
Go!
Go!
Go!

Then you start to think.

The mob overruns you,

Whoa!

Whoa!

Whoa!

You turn very pink.

Then you get real mad.

Time to snore some more.

Then you get sad.

What a bore...

Finally class is out!

The teacher lets out a sigh.

People run about,

She says, "Oh my,

oh my!"

You walk over to the teacher and give her a little pat.

She looks up at you,

and straightens up her hat.

You then walk up to your friends

Also give them a smile.

And say, Let's not bore the teacher out, not for a while!

BEYBLADES

Beyblades
They-blades
Stay-blades
Please go away-blades

Your teacher sends a letter.
It gets worse.
After you hope things get better,
they end up in a person's purse.

Your teacher asks them to go away.
This is it,
except they're here for stay!
Your happiness turns into fit.

This needs to stop,
right here,
right now.
"We can do it!"
I shout aloud

Get the badges,
cameras,
and telescopes.
Search for the Beyblades,
And tie the culprits up.
with thick brown rope.
Take them to the teacher.

Get rid of them once and for all!
Keep up hope and don't doubt!
All Beyblades must fall,
We must take this route!

Now there are only a few,
A simple number,
2,
Good enough,
for me and you.
We trust them to keep that number
and not to overdue.
Beyblades
Stay-blades
Now they went away-blades

And now we can have
a big parade!

Inspired by my fifth grade class boys' obsession with Beyblades. These are spinning tops with changeable parts. I didn't really see what the excitement was about. They had fun with these toys in and out of class. As I sat in the crowd and watched as they played every chance they got. The school rules said no toys at school. Eventually, the matter grew so big, my teacher sent a letter to all the parents. No, it didn't stop. Soon enough, my friend and I formed the "Beyblade Police". The moment we spotted a Beyblade in the classroom, we would note the time and place, it's color, and the boy. We would issue a warning or two. If the boy would not put it away, then we would tell the teacher. The Beyblade Police were partly successful, despite having only two people as members.

If Comfort Mattered More Than Happiness

If comfort mattered
more than happiness,
the world would be so dull.
No one would share a smile,
a laugh,
a joke,
a simple speech that was spoke.
Another day without the sun,
to lift the hearts of everyone.

If comfort mattered
more than happiness,
the days would be so tedious.
So long,
so dark,
an alley that never ended.
A soulless day not intended.
If comfort mattered more than happiness,

there would be mind-numbing silence.
An eerie whisper,
Lies and fibs,
the numbness of all quiet,
not comfortable at all.

So if comfort mattered more than happiness,
it wouldn't be comfort at all,
Comfort comes from happiness,
and happiness from comfort.
All for one,
and one for all.

CALL OF THE WILD

They give us food.
They let us lay.
They give us drink.
They even play.
They talk too much.
They squeeze too hard.
They scream at me,
I end up in the yard.
But every dog hears
the voice.
Wanting to run,
wanting to flee
And when you're not looking,
he will indeed.
Each paw step tells a story.
Each bark sings a song.
Each leap with majestic glory.

The wind creeps into my fur
So sleek,
So silky,
So long.
My tongue lolling out.
Then, I knew I was gone
Escaped.
Released.
Gone from canned food.
From the squeals and tight hugs.
From the chain that held me back.
From the fake large rugs.
The call out yonder,
so close, as if a magnet
Not wanting to wander,
Nearby to the forest edges.
Then that voice calls me.
Drives me into the woods.
How I left that miserable sorrow.
How I ran like I should've.
And now Wolf Brother and I,
our den more comfortable
than a man-made home.
And every distilled water-drop,

gives us the desire to roam.

Tails down.

At least a score.

Vigilant heads up.

No need for more.

The wolves gather round,

howling at the moonlit sky

I look around with belonging,

my mouth gone all too dry

The forest beckons to me.

I hear its call.

The sound of rushing leaves,

The river, strong.

I hear it like the booming cry of a child.

And now, I have touched my destiny

Because I heard the Call of the Wild

Inspired by the 2020 movie, Call of the Wild. This poem was originally written for a poetry contest.

BULLYING

Bullying,
It's not nice you see.
It's mean to other people,
and it's rude to me.

The second those words come out of their mouth
It tears them down,
down,
down.
Nearly,
almost,
down to the ground.

Bullying,
It's not nice you see.
It's mean to other people,
and it's rude to me.

Hate to see people getting hurt this way.
Hoping they'd have a better day.
Stand up for them and do what's right,
Don't give up without putting up a fight.

Bullying,
It's not nice you see.
It's mean to other people,
and it's rude to me.

Tell the teacher,
Tell 'em what they've done.
Tell 'em that bullying is wrong for everyone.

Bullying,
It's not nice you see.
It's mean to other people,
and it's rude to me.

Some people feel trapped,
like there's nowhere to run or turn,
When they go to school,
they don't wanna fight,
they wanna learn!

Because bullying,

It's not nice you see,

It's mean to other people, and it's rude to me.

A huge shout out to Bars & Melody. You are my inspiration for this poem. Bars & Melody are a pop duo that were Simon Cowell's golden buzzer act on Britain's Got Talent in 2014. Their performance against bullying, brought memories back to me of things I had seen. Then words just started popping into my head, and even better, each line I thought of rhymed.

FOREVER FRIENDS

Forever friends
through thicker and thinner,
Lunch to dinner,
Loser and winner.
Through storms and lightning.
and thunder, and all.
On the other side,
of a large brick wall.
To the ends of the earth,
From the bottom to top rack,
In the endless journey,
I know you've got my back.

We do fun things together,
Build a fort,
Hide the treasure.
It seems like fun
forever
and ever.
If I fall over,

You pick me up off the floor.
You say you've got my back,
And I say I've got yours.

IMAGINATION

We use our imagination,
Off to a faraway land.
We're pirates on a massive ship,
We're picking up seashells on the sand.
We find a magic kitten,
And nurse him back to health.
We find a box of gold,
And add it to our wealth.
We find a rare tree,
And save it before it gets cut down.
We do a monkey bar challenge,
We're over the jungle ground!
We're astronauts in space,
We've landed on the moon.
We jump around,
sing a song,
And dance to a musical tune.
We hop aboard a unicorn
and fly above the clouds.
We slide down a rainbow,

and spin around and round.
At last the night has fallen,
But our imagination isn't finished yet!

We dream of clouds made of cotton candy.
Then it rains and we get wet.
Chocolate milk is falling from the sky!
The people yell, "oh my, oh my!"
We take our cups and drink it up.
We sit on a pillow of marshmallows,
And then the sky turns from blue to ombre yellows.
We wake up and breathe in deep.
Our imagination still grows,
Even when we're not asleep.
Time for another day,
So now my friends and I can take our imagination away!

Made in the USA
Monee, IL
22 October 2020

44621054R00020